Understanding Fish Vision

Understanding Fish Vision

LAWRENCE THREADGOLD

L. T. Threadgold

COCH-Y-BONDDU BOOKS
2016

Two hundred and fifty copies of
Understanding Fish Vision
have been printed in the
Coch-y-Bonddu Books Angling Monographs Series
This copy is number . . . .
In addition there are twenty-six hardbound copies

AUTHOR'S COPY C

© Coch-y-Bonddu Books Ltd 2016
Text © Lawrence Threadgold
ISBN 978 1904784 74 6
Coch-y-Bonddu Books Ltd
Machynlleth, Powys, SY20 8DG
01654 702837
www.anglebooks.com

To my wife, Jenny

Contents

Preface

Flyfishing is an enduring pleasure and as a sport has benisons peculiar only to itself. Like any sport it can be practiced at a variety of levels and may be enjoyed as much by the tyro as by the expert. However, there is little doubt that the acquisition of knowledge about the sport will lead to increased pleasure and inward satisfaction. Acquired skills are rewarding in their own right for to fish well usually means to fish more successfully.

All sports have their magic moments; the goal, the try, the century, the long putt that drops in the cup. Flyfishing is a hunting game and so there can be no doubt that the overriding pleasure of this sport is the strike. That is the magic moment when the line goes taut and you know your skill, your experience, your general fishing nous have gained you the prize you have stalked.

Unfortunately we sometimes forget that the trout itself is a hunter of all stages from larva to adult of a variety of flying insects, not to mention larger prey such as other trout and aquatic animals. His main hunting weapon is sight. It is movement, colour, and shape which excite his predatory instincts which are, of course, themselves the simple result of hunger. But if you are going to hunt a hunter you had better have some understanding of how your prey perceives its environment, in what ways it has evolved in response to that environment which itself changes and finally what advantages, and disadvantages and limitations, its evolution has bestowed on it.

Of course trout have other senses; hearing, olfaction, taste, touch and temperature perception to mention just some. For information on these other senses see *Trout Sense* by Jason Randall (Stackpole Books, 2014) However in this text senses other than vision have been intentionally ignored as it was considered that concentrated and exclusive treatment of vision would be of the most interest to fly fishermen. The fisherman may be conscious of other trout senses but he cannot appreciate their significance in respect of fish capture when actually fishing, but the fisherman himself has vision and can observe his prey, its actions and reactions.

In this context some words of G E M Skues in his book *The Way of a Trout with a Fly* are pertinent. Skues had hoped to write a book on trout-fly dressing but concluded that 'there is one governing factor in the treatment of the subject upon which I know nothing, and upon which – so far as I can learn – the scientific knowledge of my age is unable to help me. I refer to the vision of the trout.' Happily we now have that knowledge and so can make some informed conclusions as to fly patterns and the part played by their colour, shape, etc in the success or failure in stimulating a trout to take.

This new text is based largely on Chapters 1 and 2 of my book *Dry Flies: An Improved Method of Tying* (Swan Hill Press, 1998). Consequently there will be information already known to the reader, though much of it has been greatly expanded, reinterpreted or subject to further analysis. However there will also be entirely new information giving a fresh appreciation of the subject. The overriding principal of this new text is to try to appreciate the various parameters of vision to which the trout is subjected but to do it in three dimensions, not the usual two as has been the practice of previous texts on this subject. As a consequence almost all the illustrations in this text are new and in colour and it is hoped they will give the trout fisherman a better understanding of how the trout sees and so make him a more knowledgeable hunter to his advantage and perhaps an increased pleasure from the sport of flyfishing.

Finally let me add a word of caution to the reader. The subject of vision in fish as a class of animals is naturally vast and beyond the bounds of a book such as this. Consequently it must be emphasised that the information about fish vision detailed in this book applies largely to trout and grayling and perhaps other freshwater fish but may not be applicable to other fish species such as those in marine environments.

CHAPTER ONE

Anatomy and Histology

I believe it would be advantageous to the reader of the following chapters if they were familiar with the gross anatomy and histology of the trout's eye. Without such knowledge the reader may not fully appreciate some of the nuances of the subject, what is fact and what is speculation based on limited or reasoned deductions. Unfortunately the trout cannot tell us how it sees and how it views its environment so we must gather what evidence we can and evaluate it. Nevertheless 'speculation' is not without point if it is intelligently constructed and such speculation may help us to understand the trout better and fish for it more logically.

Position of the eyes.

The trout's eyes are situated latero-frontally on the head about one third down the dorso-ventral depth of the head (Fig.1). They are more or less circular. Consequently the pupil of the eye is in line with the posterior half of the upper lips of the jaw. Viewed from the dorsal surface the eyes appear tilted towards the mid-line so that they 'see' over the downward slope of the trout's nose. From a head-on view the eyes can almost be seen in their entirety because they are tilted towards the mid-line of the head as well as being tilted slightly upwards as already mentioned. As a consequence of their positioning therefore the golden iris and pupil are obvious in head-on, overhead and of course lateral views. The importance of this positioning is considered in subsequent chapters.

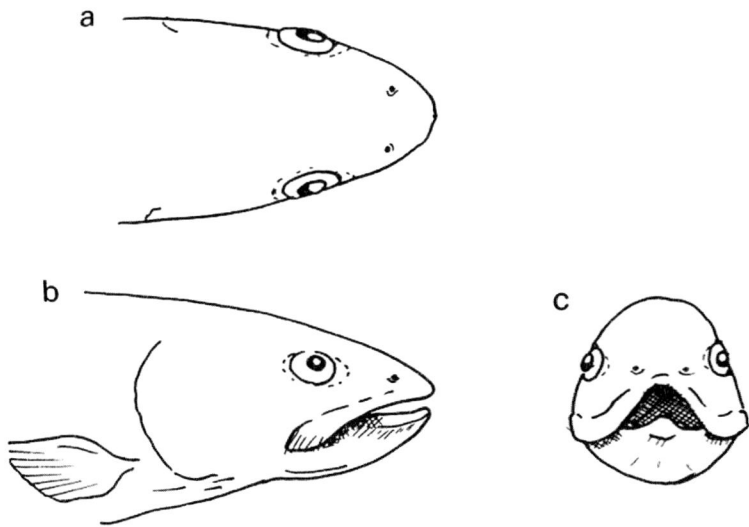

Fig.1 The position of the eyes of a trout as viewed a, from above, b, laterally and c, face on

Each eye lies in a lenticulate depression from which the eye-ball protrudes. This depression is usually ignored in texts on trout vision but recent evidence suggests the skin of the depressed lenticular region is either loose or elastic. As a result if the eye ball is rotated to look downwards it pushes upwards on the lenticular area and a 'bulge' appears as photographs by Paul Schullery, in his book *The Rise*, show (see Fig.2 A & B). Similar bulging of this region occurs when the eyeball is rotated forward, backwards or upward. Thus the eyeball has a greater ability to rotate in it socket than is usually believed. This ability to rotate within the lenticular depression allows for yaw, pitch and roll and enables the trout to stabilise any image on the retina. This would to some extent compensate for movement forced upon the trout by changes in current direction and speed, and eddies or other water movements which the trout cannot anticipate but to which it must make a response, especially if a quarry item is seen which the trout desires to capture! Whether or not the eyes can be rotated independently in different directions is not known but is within the bounds of possibility and would certainly be advantageous when hunting or avoiding predators.

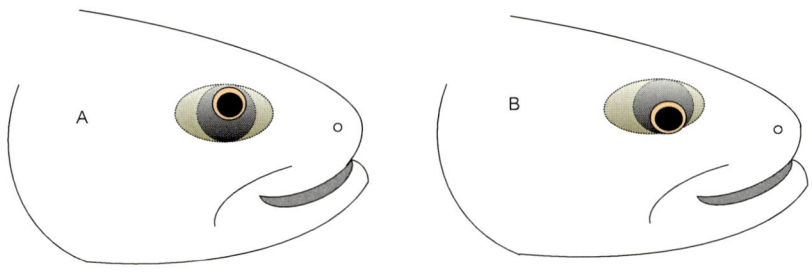

FIG.2 A) Normal position of the eye in its socket. B) Eye looking downwards and revealing an upper bulge in the eye socket. Rotating the eye in other directions would result in similar bulges opposite to the direction of rotation

Histology of the Trout's Eye

The piscean eye resembles the human eye in many aspects but differs in some important anatomical features. The cornea is translucent, slightly curved and continuous with the cartilaginous sclera which forms the hemispherical back of the eye. The cornea is covered externally by a clear layer of skin which includes the conjunctiva. The cornea does not act as the first focusing unit of the eye as it does in humans, for whom the lens is a secondary device which ensures fine definition of objects.

A further difference between the human and trout eye is that the lens is not 'lenticular shaped' but spherical. However for trout, Sosin & Clark in *Through the Fish's Eye* suggest that the lens may be egg-shaped with the pointed end aimed at the retina. However for purposes of this text the generally accepted view that the lens of a trout's eye is a sphere will be accepted. The lens is suspended by an elastic ligament above (the suspensory ligament Fig.3) and a retractable muscle below (the retractor lentis muscle in Fig.3). The lens is composed of living cells and encapsulated by a very thin layer of other cells so that it grows in parallel with the trout itself. The lens has a very short focal length of approximately 2.5 times its radius. The front face of the lens projects slightly through the iris which generally appears as a golden ring round the dark centre of the eye and so lies close to the cornea. Consequently the anterior chamber of the eye is very small.

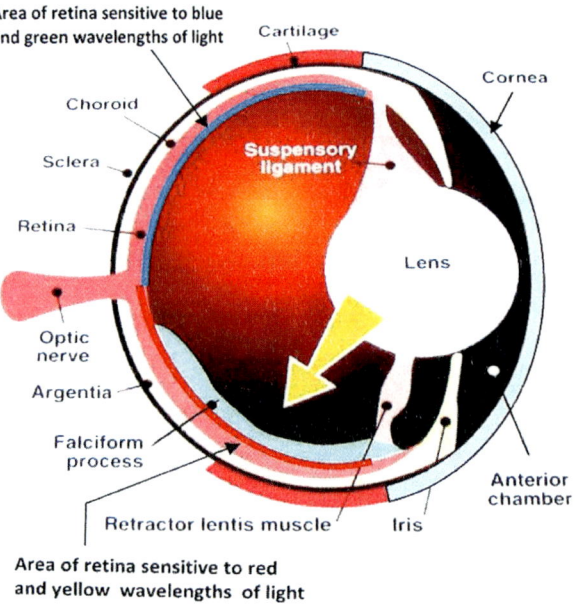

Area of retina sensitive to blue
and green wavelengths of light

Cartilage

Cornea

Choroid

Suspensory
ligament

Sclera

Retina

Lens

Optic
nerve

Argentia

Falciform
process

Anterior
chamber

Retractor lentis muscle

Iris

Area of retina sensitive to red
and yellow wavelengths of light

Fig.3 Vertical section of the eye of a trout. Note the retractor lentis muscle and the large yellow arrow pointing to the general direction in which the lens moves when the retractor lentis muscle contracts during focussing

The lens is not homogeneous and so has a different refractive index in different parts ensuring that the light rays passing though the lens all focus on the same point on the retina (Fig.4A). The highest refractive index is in the centre of the lens and falls off progressively to the periphery. Consequently the lens does not show Spherical Aberration, i.e., a situation where light rays passing through different part of the lens do not all focus at the same point on the retina (Fig.4B). The lens is uncorrected for Chromatic Aberration, that is light of different wavelengths (colours) will not all focus at the same point on the retina. Presumably the trout's brain can cope with this fact and somehow corrects it neurologically to give a correct image of the object seen or perhaps to mask out such an abnormality.

As already mentioned, the anterior chamber is limited by the iris which is an opaque ring of tissue which block out light, especially from the trout's peripheral vision. However it has a fixed aperture

16

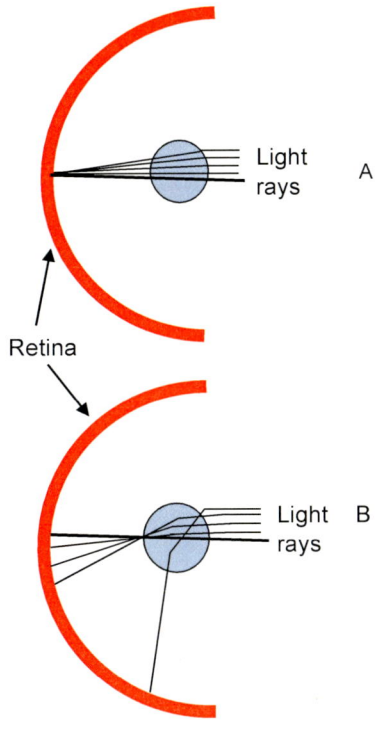

Retina

and cannot 'close' and 'open' as it does in humans. This facility in humans allows control of the amount of light reaching the retina and so helps visual acuity by reducing glare and the scattering of light within the eye; this function is unavailable to trout. However in bright sunlight there are alterations in the light sensitivity of the retina cells which are of three types, the pigment cells, the rods and the cones, The pigment cells occur between the latter two types of cells and in bright light the pigment granules they contain migrate to the surface of these cells and so reduce the amount of light received by the other cells, reduce scattering of light within the retina and so protects the rods and cones from damage (see later in this chapter).

Fig.4 A) The different refractive indices in different parts of the spherical lens of a trout, (blue sphere), ensures a focus on the retina. B) Lack of focus (spherical aberration) which would result if the refractive index of all parts of the lens were the same

Naturally the facts just stated induce certain behavioural patterns in trout. In very bright sunlight trout tend to seek shade under the shadows thrown by the adjacent vegetation, or lie close to the bank or weed clumps. Thus they are better able to see the water surface and anything on it. Lying deeper in the water would have a similar effect especially if the water was 'coloured' due to suspended solids or other impurities of various kinds, which is the usual situation in both rivers and lakes. These impurities scatter the light and result in 'cloudiness' which can greatly reduce the visual compass of the trout. Sosin and Clark state that 'In murky lakes most of the light is gone in the first ten feet. Still, if sunshine is illuminating the surface at 2,000 foot candles there will be twenty foot candles at the depth where only one percent of light remains, plenty of light for trout to feed by.' These authors also state that this turbidity 'reduces visibility to between five and forty feet.'

In view of this behaviour in the seeking of shade or depth, the activity of the pigment cells and the turbidity of water has consequences for the fly, the trout and fisherman. Under such circumstances it would obviously be wise to change tactics by casting in the margins, increasing the depth at which nymphs are fished and perhaps use flies incorporating shiny or flashy reflective materials, such as gold-heads or mylar.

The iris is continuous with a silvery layer, the argentea which lines the inside of the sclera. (Fig.3). This layer can be important in some fish as it reflects light back into the retinal cells, so aiding vision in poor light. Between this silvery layer and the retina is the choroid, a complex of blood vessels which supplies oxygen and nutrients to the retina. Near the entrance of the optic nerve at the back of the eye, a vascular fold of the choroid, the falciform process, penetrates the retina, crosses the posterior chamber and ends as a knob attached to the back of the lens; it presumably supplies oxygen and other chemicals such as ions necessary to a living and continually growing lens.

As already stated, the lens does not alter shape during focussing as it does in the human eye. Instead the lens is moved closer to the retina by means of the retractor lentis muscle (Fig.3: the yellow arrow). However this simple statement must be subject to further comment because;

1. The retina is slightly ellipsoidal since its anterior-posterior axis (front to back) is some 3% longer than the vertical one.

2. The contraction of the retractor lentis muscle moves the lens not towards the centre of the retina but backwards almost parallel to the anterior-posterior axis of the trout's body.

In a reasonably sized trout the semi-elliptical retina is 10.3 mm along the major axis, (front to back), and 10.0 mm along the minor axis, (top to bottom). The centre of the spherical lens at rest is about

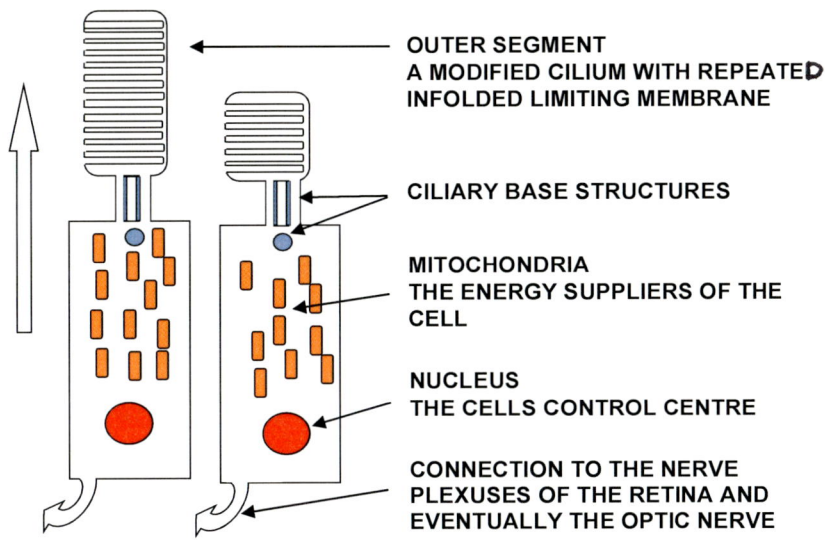

Fig.5 *Diagrammatic representation of a rod and a cone. The infolds are more numerous than shown and more closely packed. The rod has a shorter outer segment than the cone. The cones are not always single as some are double. Arrow at left shows direction of the light*

5.0 mm from the anterior margins of the retina but 5.3 mm from the posterior part of the retina. (Example taken from R J Pumphrey. See References). When the lentis muscle contracts it pulls the lens towards the temporal quadrant of the retina and so brings remove objectives ahead and above into focus. The distance of the lens to the remainder of the retina is virtually unchanged; consequently no focusing is possible for other directions of view.

The retina forms the innermost layer of the eye and so lines the posterior chamber. It contains two types of light receptor cells.

The rods which detect only in black shading to grey and then white, are about 30 times more sensitive than cones and so respond well to dim light. They are therefore important in the detection of contrast and movement.

The cones are more effective in bright light and detect colour and detail. Consequently they are more active in daylight or 'whenever the light level is brighter than one foot candle.' (Sosin & Clark, 1976).

The rod and cone cells have a similar structure and consist of three parts, the outer segment, the stalk and the cell body. The outer segment is derived from a cilium, a hair-like protrusion from the cell surface. In certain cells the cilium can move back and forth or make other complex movements. However in the photoreceptive cell the cilium is highly modified. Its limiting membrane (plasma membrane) is repeatedly folded inwards, so that the outer segment appears like a pile of coins (shown in the upper part of Fig.5).

In humans the cones are restricted to a small area (the fovea) but in trout they are widely distributed over the retina so forming a mosaic with the rods. The reason for this is that trout cannot readily move the head from side to side or up and down. Furthermore the trout's eye has relatively more rods than cones and so works better in dim light than the human eye. It is also very responsive to movement and contrast but is not so capable at discerning fine detail and subtle differences in shades of colour. The rods are consequently sometimes called grey-scale vision. For protection, in bright light the rods are physically retracted into the pigment layer, i.e., away from the posterior chamber and the direction of light. In poor light the rods are moved towards the posterior chamber and nearer the light source so as to be more effective. The cones react in the opposite to the rods being nearer the light source in daylight and retreating into the pigment layer at night.

Trout vision must therefore be subject to a diurnal cycle with the cones obviously dominating during daylight and the rods at night. The change-over takes place slowly but must be reset daily to fit in with the natural changes in the length of daytime and night-time during the year. Consequently the trout must have an internal circadian rhythm (clock), which anticipates the ever changing times of dawn and dusk. What stimulus or hormone is responsible for the daily resetting of the clock is unknown. The trout's eye is therefore well adapted to an environment in which light penetrates less well than in air. The trout's milieu is often cloudy or hazy and disturbed by currents and other water movements.

The neural parts of the light-receptor cells of the retina, (also called photo-receptors) and the intermediate nerve cells and plexuses which line the inner face of the posterior chamber connect the retina to the brain by exiting just below the centre of the back of the eye-ball as the optic nerve. This arrangement is surprising for it is natural to expect the photo-receptor cells to line the posterior chamber and the other nerves and plexuses to be behind, rather than in front. This is because the vertebrate eye is inverted with the nerve cells which conduct impulses to the brain being nearer to the lens than the photo-receptors which actually perceive and respond to light rays. During development of the eye, it appears first as a stalked, bulbous outgrowth of the forebrain but as it grows the front of the ball folds inwards to form a double layer with the back wall; hence the eye is inverted. The stalk becomes the optic nerve.

Trout are trichromatic, i.e., they have cones sensitive to blue, green and yellow/red. These may be in a matrix; for example blue cones surrounded by green or orange yellow. Some cones have pigments which absorb light of short wavelengths (blues and greens) and others pigments which absorb light with long wavelengths (yellow, orange and red). The first class of pigment predominates in the upper part of the retina and so this part is adapted to looking at the substrate and its vegetation, that is at objects where blues and greens predominate (Fig.3). The second class of pigments predominates in the lower part of the retina and so is adapted to looking upwards and responding to the longer wavelengths.

Sosin & Clark (1976) have an interesting table (Fig.5A) concerning the depth at which colours of different wavelengths penetrate on the assumption that the water has clarity. What is the significance of the

Penetration of Light of Different Wavelengths With Water Depth			
COLOUR	10 FEET	20 FEET	30 FEET
RED	6.50%	0.40%	0.03%
ORANGE	50%	25%	12%
YELLOW	73%	53%	40%
GREEN	88%	78%	69%

Fig.5A

table to the fly fisherman? Obviously with depth a fly with orange would be more readily visible than one in red and yellow would be even more visible.

Though green is the most visible at depth it will also be closest to vegetation growing from the substratum and so may lose some of its advantages as it is surrounded by other greens. At depth yellow is clearly the best colour for a fly and the effectiveness of the fly may be increased by touches of orange. It would be interesting to discover the penetrating ability of a black/white combination in a fly, which should be more visible to the rods than the cones.

There is another concern for the flyfisher regarding the colouring of a river or lake. As every watercolour painter knows, a thin wash over a base colour can alter that base colour considerably. If the base is red then a green wash will turn it towards brown, or if it is a yellow base then the yellow will turn to a bright yellow-green. Similarly for blue, the green wash would result in a very deep green and with a brown wash the blue would become darker and approach black.

What is the importance of these colour changes due to coloured water for the fisherman? Most chalk streams are clear and so will have little effect of the colour of a sunken fly. However even these rivers can be in spate and appear a moderate brown colour or even greenish under certain conditions; lakes can suffer equally. Consequently the colours of a sunken artificial fly will not be as bright as they appeared on the bench and may be dulled or brightened by the 'coloured wash' of the water in which they are immersed. This fact may account for artificial flies being ignored as they are the 'wrong' colour or are not as conspicuous and as stimulating to the trout's appetite as we might expect!

It should be pointed out that the foregoing descriptions of colour vision in trout relates largely to those trout inhabiting relatively shallow waters such as rivers or lakes and consequently the facts in this text are most applicable to trout and grayling, the flyfisher's quarry. However, there is wide variation in the features mentioned as trout have adapted to different environments, for example those in oceans, those occupying great depth where light is very poor, and those in very shallow waters such a pools on a shore. Some trout can appreciate ultra-violet, though this facility may be lost in an adult. The variations in a trout's visual abilities are therefore as diverse as the different species of trout. Obviously vision in trout as a group of animals is a vast subject and inappropriate for this text.

CHAPTER TWO

A Trout's View of its Underwater Environment

The positioning and the physical characteristics of the trout's eyes in relation to its vision.

The positioning of the trout's eyes in relation to its body has a profound influence on its perception of its underwater surroundings and also impinges on its perception of the above water world as described in the subsequent chapter.

As already stated the eyes are positioned latero-frontally and inclined slightly inward and upwards and the lens is spherical. This gives the trout a field of view in each eye of 180° (Fig.6). These two fields overlap in front and consequently the trout's field of vision is subdivided into three sectors. There are two large lateral sectors of monocular vision each of about 145° and a single narrow sector of binocular vision in front and overhead of between 28–35 degrees (Figs 7 & 8).

Monocular vision

When viewed from directly in front the monocular sectors are 166°. When viewed from directly overhead the monocular sectors start at 17.5° posterior to the anterio-posterior line (nose to tail) and therefore forms left and right monocular sectors of 162.5°. In the monocular sectors the trout can, to quote R J Pumphrey, 'be assumed to have adequate vision for large objects at all distances with

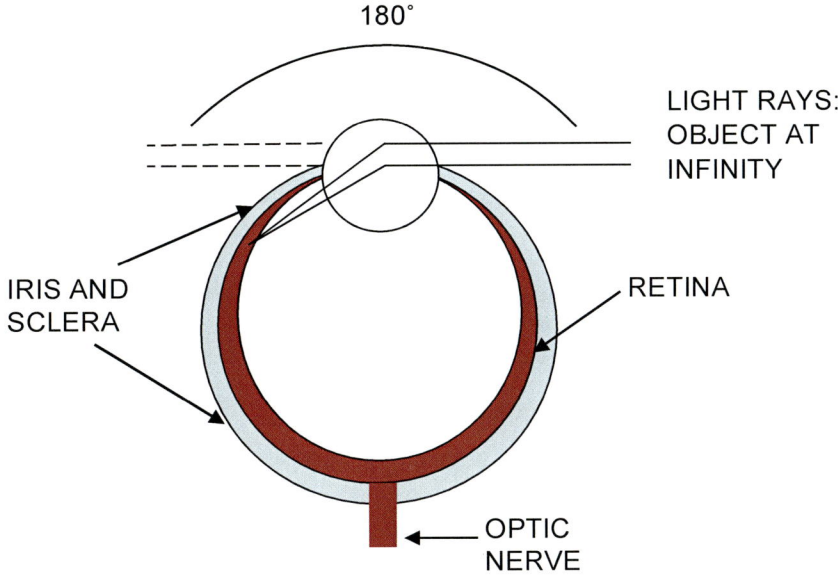

Fig.6 Diagrammatic drawing of a trout's eye to show that the spherical lens allows a sector of vision of 180°

its unaccommodated eye.' In other words the eye has a depth of field, (the horizontal distance over which all objects are in focus), in the monocular sectors as if focused at infinity. Consequently, focussing is not required for these monocular sectors. Indeed it is not possible to focus these sectors due to the backward direction the lens travels when the retractor lentis muscle contracts. Trout to all intents and purposes appears to have only a right and a left monocular sector.

Binocular vision

Due to the disposition of its eyes the trout has binocular vision both overhead and in front. The binocular sector has an angle of 28° when viewed from head-on (Fig.7) while seen from above the angle is about 35° (Fig.8); both angles are approximate to within a couple of degrees. Experiments suggest that viewed from the side, binocular vision extends from 25° below the horizontal to 100° above it giving a sector of 125° (Figs 9 & 10).

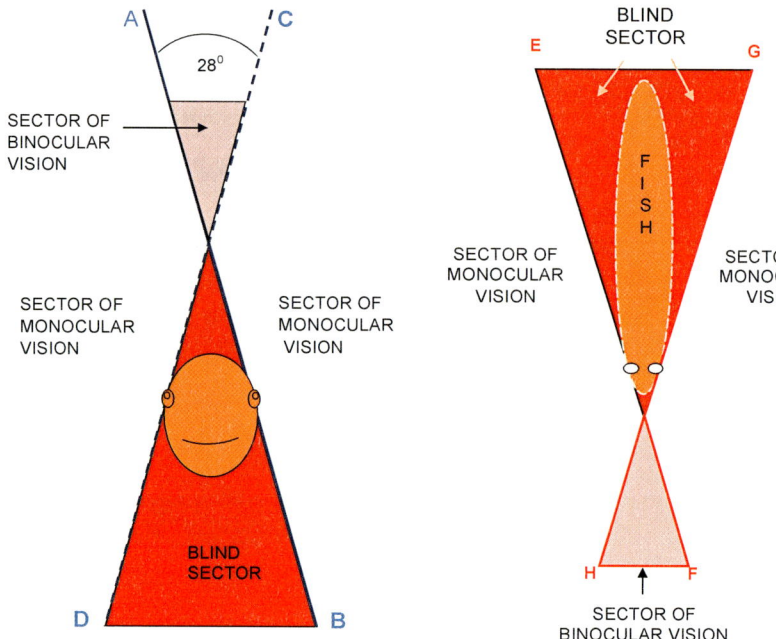

Fig.7 Sectors of binocular and monocular vision as viewed from directly in front. The red area is the blind sectors immediately above and below the trout's head and will extend to the substratum. Other sectors have undefined limits but will come up against the mirror as the trout sees it (see later)

Fig.8 Sectors of binocular and monocular vision when viewed from directly overhead. The red area indicates the blind sector both in front of and behind the trout. The extent of the binocular sector may be limited by the mirror as may the rear of the blind area. The extent of the sectors of monocular vision is undefined but will eventually impinge on the mirror as the trout sees it (see later)

A three dimensional illustration of the possible relationship of the monocular, and binocular sectors of the two windows and their accompanying mirrors and the trout is shown in Fig.11. Although it is not known if sector C also runs down the inner surface of the two mirrors, it may do so for a short distance; at present there is no evidence either way.

When the eye is unaccommodated (at rest) the elliptical shape of the retina ensures the trout is myopic (short-sighted) in its binocular sectors. To quote J R Pumphrey, 'the trout can see clearly with an unaccommodated eye objects just in front of its nose of the size class

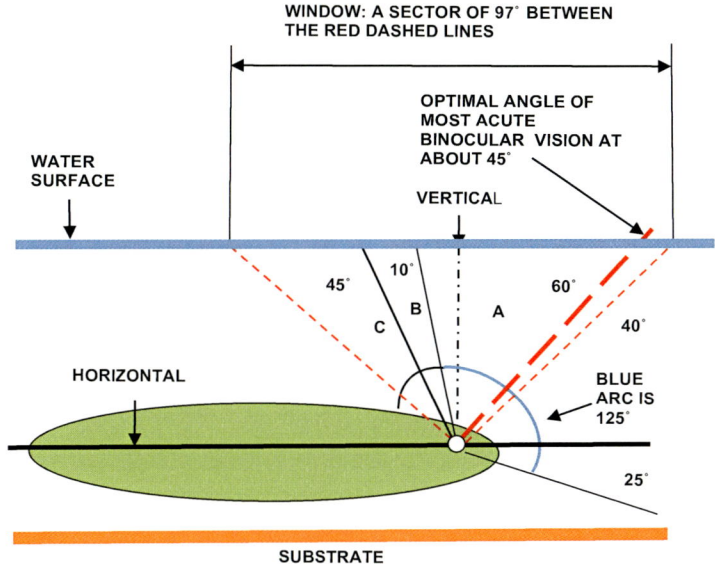

WINDOW: A SECTOR OF 97° BETWEEN
THE RED DASHED LINES

OPTIMAL ANGLE OF
MOST ACUTE
BINOCULAR VISION AT
ABOUT 45°

WATER
SURFACE

VERTICAL

45°   10°

60°

B   A

C   40°

HORIZONTAL

BLUE
ARC IS
125°

25°

SUBSTRATE

Fig.9 Side view of sectors of binocular vision

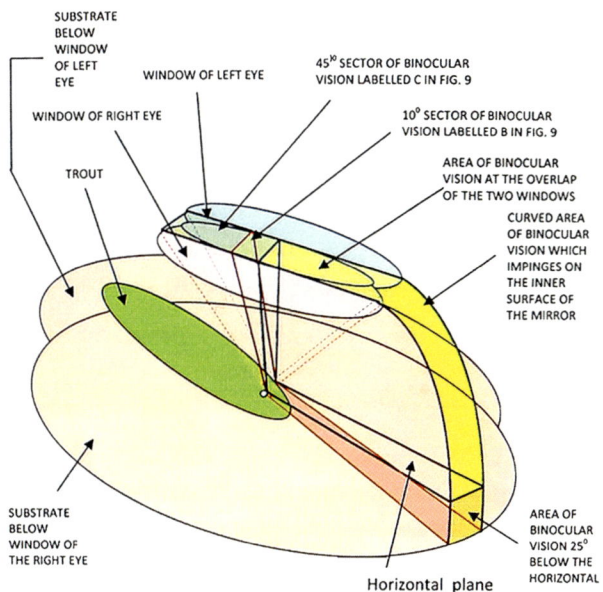

SUBSTRATE
BELOW
WINDOW
OF LEFT
EYE

WINDOW OF LEFT EYE

45° SECTOR OF BINOCULAR
VISION LABELLED C IN FIG. 9

WINDOW OF RIGHT EYE

10° SECTOR OF BINOCULAR
VISION LABELLED B IN FIG. 9

AREA OF BINOCULAR
VISION AT THE OVERLAP
OF THE TWO WINDOWS

TROUT

CURVED AREA
OF BINOCULAR
VISION WHICH
IMPINGES ON
THE INNER
SURFACE OF
THE MIRROR

SUBSTRATE
BELOW
WINDOW OF
THE RIGHT EYE

AREA OF
BINOCULAR
VISION 25°
BELOW THE
HORIZONTAL

Horizontal plane

*Fig.10 Three dimensional illustration of the sectors of binocular vision based on Fig.9. The
two mirrors surrounding the two windows have been ignored for the sake of clarity, but see
later in the chapter. Diagrammatic and not to scale*

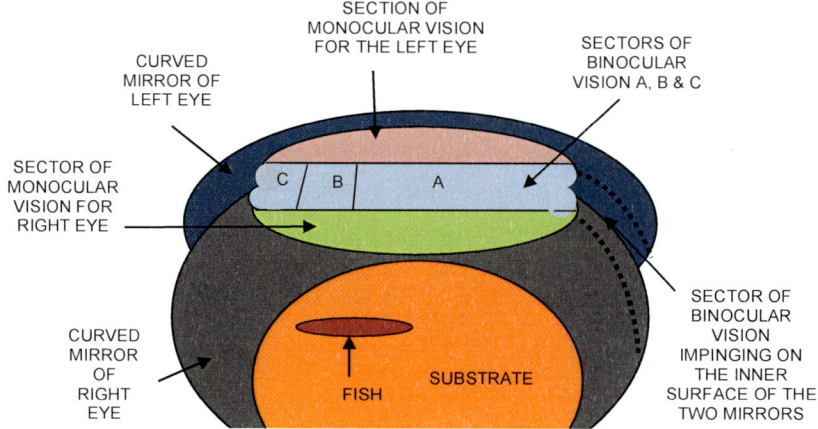

Fig.11 Illustration of the sectors of monocular and binocular vision surrounded by the two curved mirrors. The front of the nearer curved mirror has been cut away to reveal the trout and the substrate. The 'cloak' surrounding the trout has also been removed. Not to scale. The reason for showing the two mirrors as curved is explained in Chapter 4

for which a child would have to accommodate strongly and an old man would have to use an accessory lens.' However, vision of remote objects ahead is severely limited. Pumphrey states that 'clear vision is limited to objects at a distance of 10–20 cms (about 4–12 inches). At greater distances increased blurring of the image and decreasing angular subtense work together to prevent objects being clearly seen.' In a predator such as the trout the contraction of the well-developed retractor lentis muscle brings into focus on the temporal part of the retina remote objects in front and overhead; these objects are presumably located in the 125° sector of binocular vision (Figs 9 & 10).

Binocular vision and blind spots.

When the trout is looked at from in front and from above it becomes clear that there are zones of monocular and binocular vision and also zones where the trout is 'blind' simply because of the positioning of its eyes (Figs 7 & 8).

When combined in a three dimensional model the blind spots would appear as a sort of 'cloak' with only the eyes outside (Fig.12).

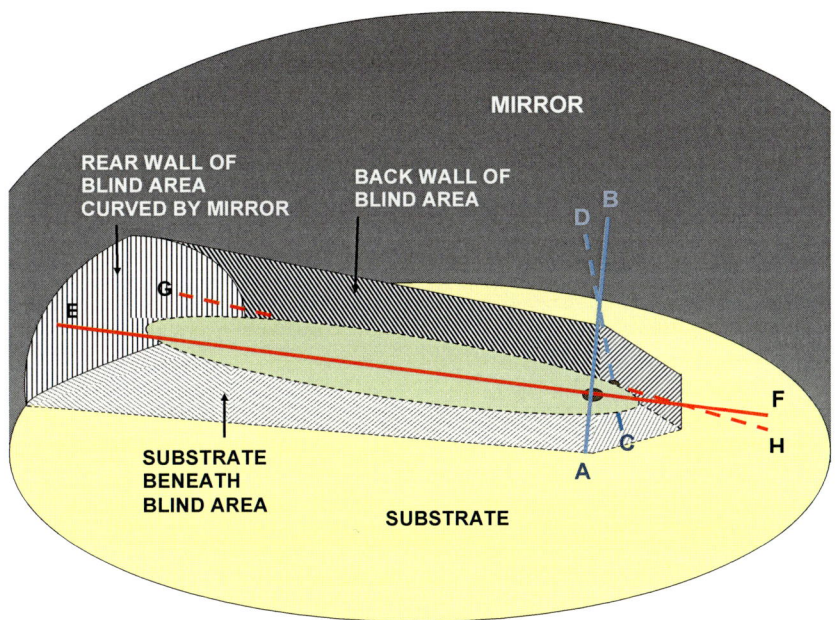

Fig.12 A possible three dimensional representation of the 'blind' area surrounding a trout. The left-hand (side nearest to observer) has been removed to reveal the interior. A-B and C-D are the same blue lines as in Fig.7 and E-F and G-H are the same red lines as in Fig.8. The substrate should be two interlocking circles due to the fact that the trout has a visual bowl for each eye as shown in Fig.11 and as explained in Chapters 3 and 4

The idea that the trout is surrounded by a cloak-like area, which it cannot appreciate and does not know is there, may seem unbelievable. However a little thought reveals that blind spots in an animal's visual landscape are not unusual, indeed may be said to be almost universal in higher species. We have only to think of ourselves to have a perfect example. We cannot see the features of our own face, except the tip of our nose if we squint, or our tongue and lower lip if we stick them out. We cannot see our neck, our ears, the back of our head or our dorsal (back) almost down to the buttocks. Consequently we are covered by a cloak-like blind area which virtually covers our head and we can only see the backs of our thighs and lower legs by turning our body and head to awkward angles that we cannot maintain for long.

Fig.12 is to some degree not a true reflection of the trout's 'cloak.' In the drawing the end wall of the 'cloak' appears as a smooth curved area going from left to right. However it may also curve from top to bottom, a matter dealt with in Chapter 4. It must be appreciated that there is movement of the blind-area cloak as we turn our heads. If we turn our heads as far as we can to the right the cloak moves round to the left and we cannot see our left shoulder and upper arm clearly; the opposite is also true. In view of the fact that trout can only bend their necks a limited amount and neither can they move their neck up or down to any degree, their blind area will not move in a greater arc than ours. However we now know that trout can move their eyes freely within the depressed area which surrounds them and it may be possible that their blind-area cloak may also move but this is not known for sure. Another uncertainty about the cloak is what happens when the trout changes depth. Does the bottom of the cloak always stay in contact with the substratum or does it go progressively under the ventral surface of the body, though never in contact with it? Our cloak seems to us to go to infinity and perhaps the trout experiences the same effect.

CHAPTER THREE

A Trout's View of its Above-water Environment

With knowledge of the underwater vision of the trout the reader is able to proceed to an understanding of the trout's perception of its surroundings above the water surface. The trout's appreciation of its environment is governed by two things; refraction, that is the bending of light rays as they pass between media of different densities, and the positioning of their eyes in relation to their body.

Light rays show no bending in their path as they travel through air and then water if the rays are vertical to the horizontal water surface.

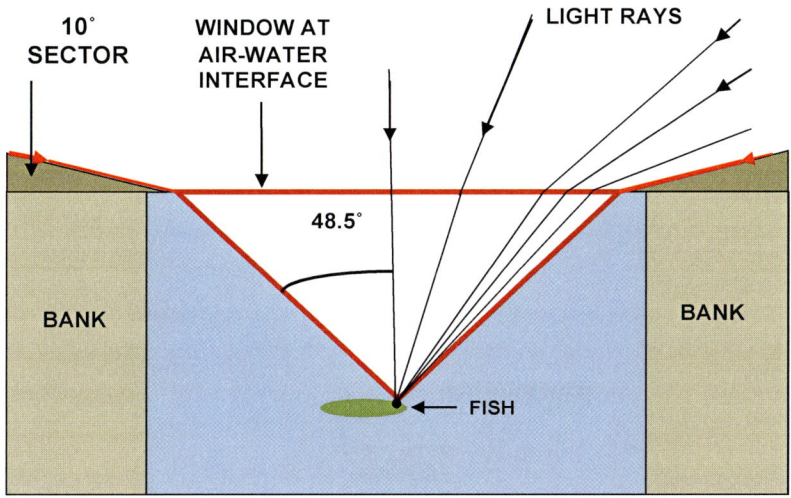

Fig.13 The trout's 160° arc of vision above the water surface is funnelled down to 97° below the water surface due to refraction. Below 100° from the horizontal is a virtual blind spot

However rays entering from other angles show increasing refraction until 10° is reached. Rays entering the water below 10° have such a small amount of light, and the image above the water is so distorted, that this angle may be considered a limiting one for the trout's view of the world above the water surface. The only images which are useful to the trout are those emanating from structures more than 10° above the horizontal (Fig.13).

As a consequence of refraction between air and water the trout has a cone of vision with an angle of 97° at its tip which is located at the trout's eye. The base of the cone impinges on the water surface

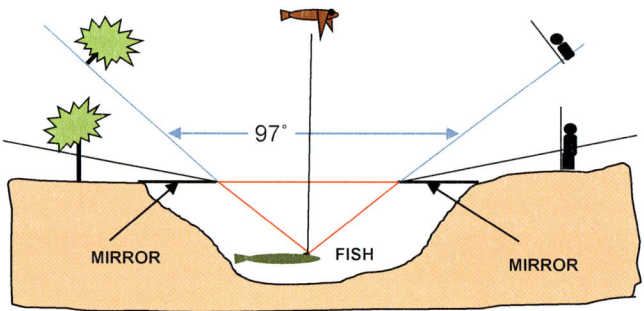

Fig.14 The trout's view of its surroundings. The bird appears true to size and shape. The fisherman and tree appear uphill along a projection (blue line) of the underwater 48.5° limits to the trout's cone of vision (red triangle)

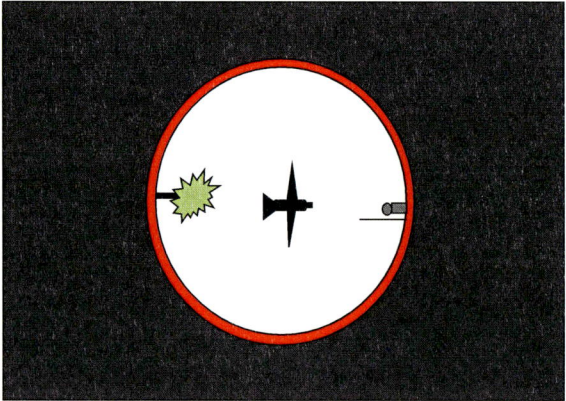

Fig.15 The trout's view through its window. This view is not strictly true; see opposite

as a circular area called 'Snell's Window', because it serves just that purpose to the trout who therefore can see anything on the bank higher than 10°, though images will become more 'blurred' as 10° is approached. Above the water surface the visual cone widens to an angle of 160° (the horizontal 180° less 10° for each side).

However to the trout this increased angle is of no importance since its visual cone of only 97° means its maximum line of sight is at 48.5°. Therefore to the trout a tree on the bank or a fisherman would appear to be projected 'uphill' into the sky (Fig.14). Rays of light with an angle exceeding 48.5° are reflected back into the water and so the water surface acts as a mirror from the trout's view (Fig.14). This topic is considered later in this chapter.

However the two dimensional illustrations above give an entirely wrong impression of how the trout sees the above-water world. These illustrations cover one eye only and of course the trout has two. A three dimensional view of the trout shows the two windows overlap. Consequently for the trout the window is not a single circular area but as viewed from above is more like a figure 8 laid sideways as in Fig.16 below. The extent of this overlap (which is presumed to give binocular vision) varies in size depending on two things, the depth

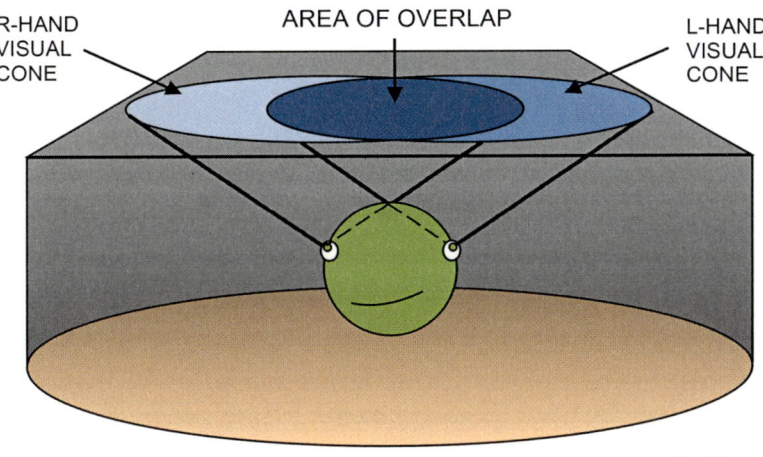

Fig.16

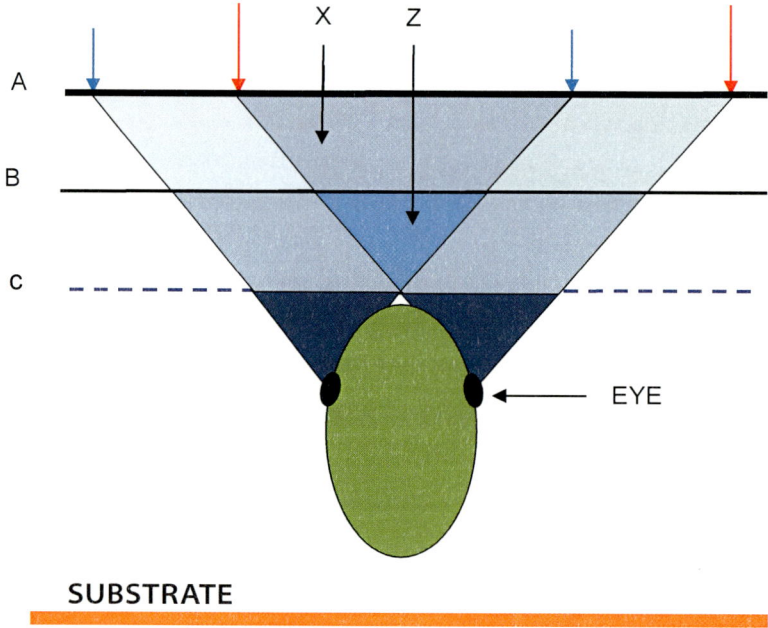

SUBSTRATE

Fig.17 A, B and C represent different water levels above the substrate. The blue arrows are the limits of the visual cone of the right eye and the red arrows the limits of the visual cone of the left eye. X points to the overlap of the two visual cones when the water level is at A; Z points to the reduced overlap of the two visual cones when the water level is at B (darker blue triangle). When the water level is at C there is no overlap (small white inverted triangle)

the trout lies in the water (Fig.17) and the distance between the eyes of the trout (Fig.18).

As previously mentioned in Fig.14 the circular window is surrounded by an area called the 'mirror'. This mirror is formed because any ray of light emanating from the trout's eye with an angle in excess of 48.5° from the vertical is reflected back into the water and so the underside of the water surface acts in essence like a mirror (Fig.19).

In tank experiments this mirror is usually light to dark grey or, if the base of the tank is coloured as would be the case if it was wooden, it takes on a tinge of the wood colour. A silvered or more or less uniformly coloured surface are probably not those the trout sees.

Its mirror would reflect the substratum, stones, weeds, etc. so the result is some combination of greens and browns and a variety

34

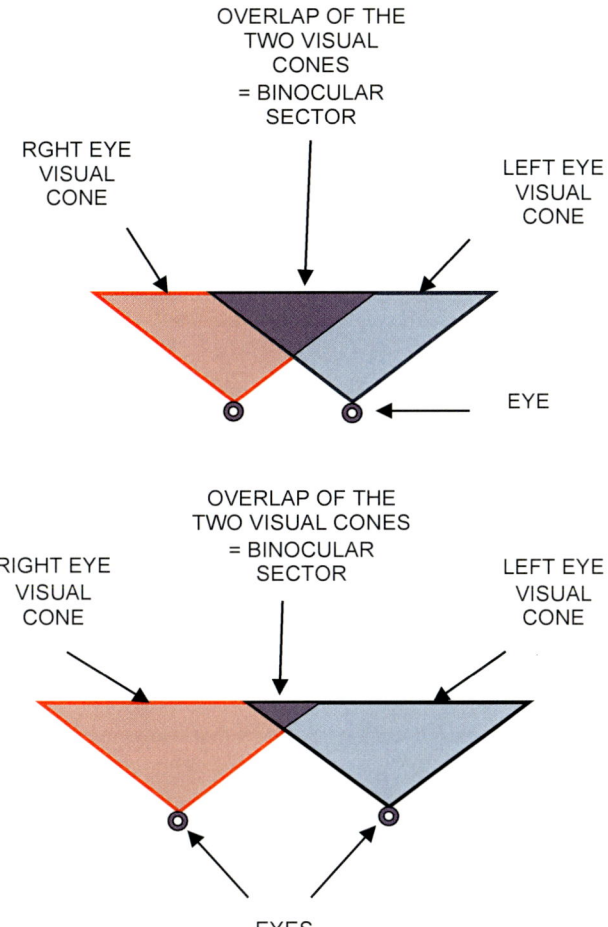

OVERLAP OF THE
TWO VISUAL
CONES
= BINOCULAR
SECTOR

RGHT EYE
VISUAL
CONE

LEFT EYE
VISUAL
CONE

EYE

OVERLAP OF THE
TWO VISUAL CONES
= BINOCULAR
SECTOR

RIGHT EYE
VISUAL
CONE

LEFT EYE
VISUAL
CONE

EYES

Fig.18   Differences in the width of overlap in two trout of different sizes but lying at the same depth, (about 2.0 cm) in relation to the water surface The smaller upper trout has eyes about 2.0 cm apart resulting in a large area of overlap whilst the lower trout has eyes about 3.5 cm apart which greatly reduces the overlap area. The trout's window is 2.26 x the depth at which the trout lies. A doubling of the depth results in a quadrupling of the size of the window

of shapes and shades of these features. Consequently, for the trout the mirror ranges from white through blue, green and brown and admixtures of all these. The mirror seen in an aquarium of static water is not the usual colour of the mirror in nature and therefore the term is a misnomer but is now an adopted term in trout fishing. Finally the mirror is an unstable ceiling limited by whatever boundaries

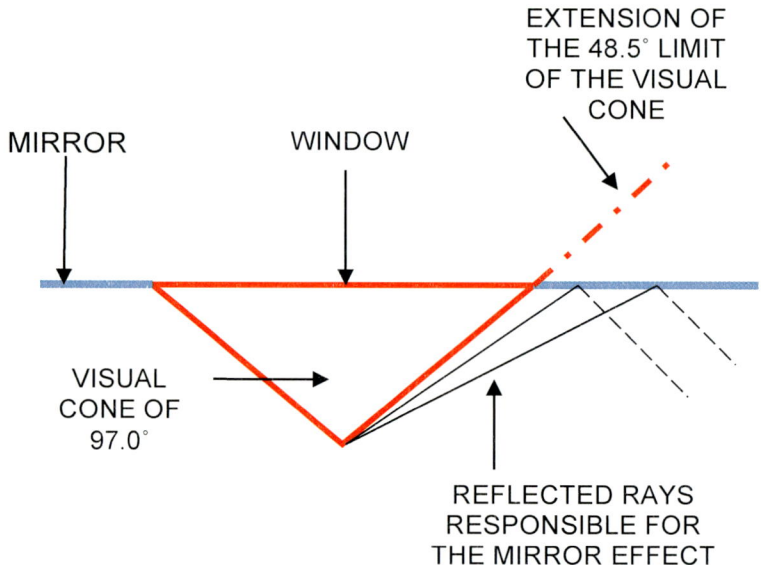

EXTENSION OF
THE 48.5° LIMIT
OF THE VISUAL
CONE

MIRROR   WINDOW

VISUAL
CONE OF
97.0°

REFLECTED RAYS
RESPONSIBLE FOR
THE MIRROR EFFECT

Fig.19 Formation of the mirror by light rays reflected from the underside of the water surface. The blue lines represent the 'flat' mirror at the surface but, as explained later in the text, the trout does not see a 'flat' mirror

surrounds the water. It is not uniform because of the effects of wind, and currents and flotsam.

There is another important detail about the mirror. The trout does not see a more or less flat mirror. To the trout the mirror is a curved screen sloping to an horizon in the middle distance (Fig.20). The slope of the screen and its extent will be a result of the depth of the water and the depth that the trout lies within this body of water (see Chapter 4 for more detail on this important topic). To be surrounded with these shallow bowls, one for each eye and which overlap in the centre may seem odd at first sight but a comparison with our own surroundings is pertinent.

If we were standing in a featureless landscape we would feel as though we were within an inverted bowl, the sky, which would seem to curve down on every side until it reached the horizon (Fig.21). Clouds though at the same height in the sky would appear to curve downwards and become smaller as the horizon is approached. A series of posts would appear to become smaller with distance and the

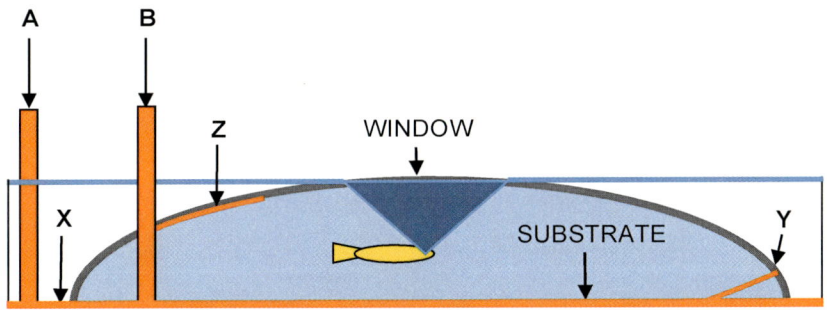

Fig.20 Cross-section of an area of water showing the surroundings of the trout. The inverted visual cone and window are in dark blue, the curving mirror, as the trout sees it (see later in text), and the 'horizon' where mirror and ground meet (X or Y). A is a post beyond the horizon and so invisible to the trout. B is a post within the 'silvered bowl' and is reflected on it at Z

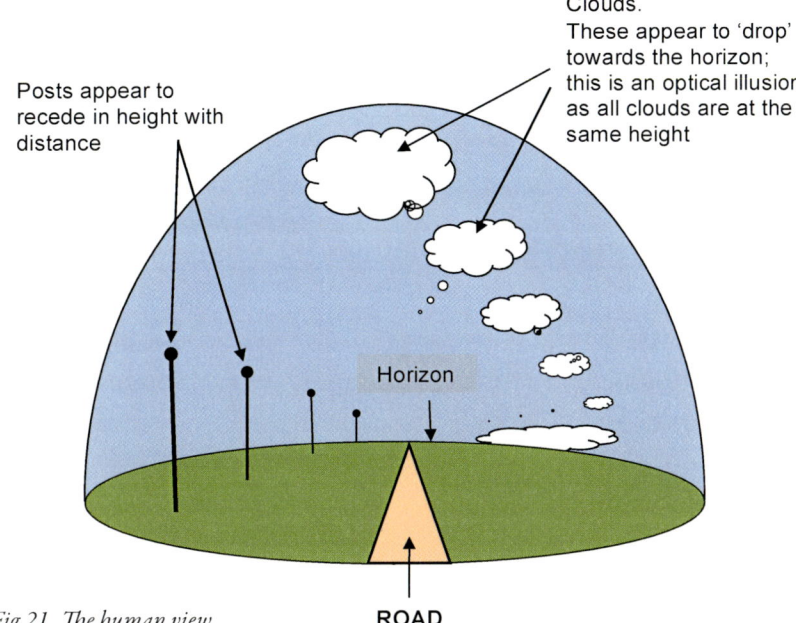

Fig.21 The human view

roads would appear to narrow and disappear. Anything below the horizon would be invisible to us. All this is an optical illusion since we know the 'sky' is not a limiting roof but goes to infinity, the clouds are all at the same height in the sky and the posts all the same height. Of course a featureless landscape is rare as vegetation, buildings and other features may obstruct our view of the horizon and become more like a landscape or picture frame. Nevertheless this apparent inverted bowl is always over us and it is an illusion which cannot be changed.

There is another point about human vision which must be mentioned. Though we sense we are in a single 'bowl,' our left and right eyes actually see different and limited parts of the environment. In essence we too have two bowls! If it were not so we would not have binocular vision and be able to judge distance. However our brain integrates these two views into a single overall view of our environment.

There is the possibility that the same is true for trout. Since their eyes are situated laterally and so each eye has its own silvered bowl, these bowls overlap to give binocular vision. Could it be that the trout's brain integrates these two bowls into one and so the trout sees its world very much as we see ours?

There is another aspect of the window/mirror relationship which is often ignored or unmentioned. The boundary between the two is often depicted as a sharp one as in Fig.15. However the boundary is in fact blurred because some light enters at and below 10°. This results in an iridescent circle called 'Snell's Circle' which appears like a rainbow with red nearest the mirror followed by orange, yellow, green, blue, and violet. The orange and yellow bands are usually the most significant (Fig.22). Snell's Window is therefore separated from the mirror by Snell's Circle. The clarity of the circle is subject to the smoothness or otherwise of the water surface being most sharp in a flat calm and ill-defined when the water is turbulent.

Is there any advantage to a fly fisherman knowing about Snell's Circle? There are some indications that trout respond well to flies which have yellow or orange in their construction. The wings of most mayflies and other insects of interest to trout are fairly translucent. Consequently as the fly approaches the window the well known sequence of events occurs. The trout first sees the sparkle of the insect's feet in the mirror, followed by the gradual appearance of the wings and finally the uniting of the images of the feet and

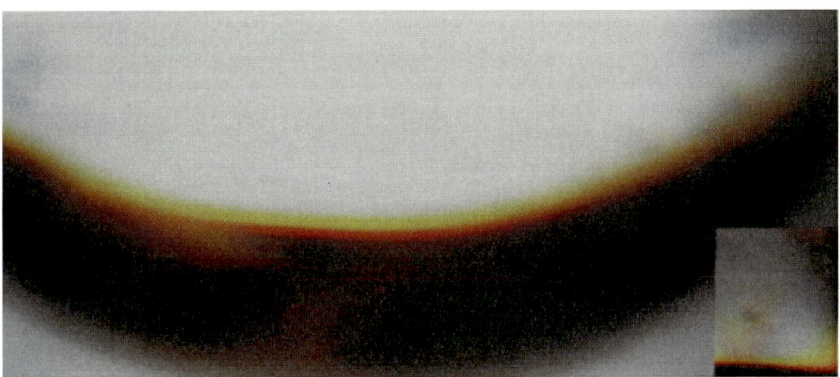

Fig.22 Snell's Circle. The mirror is at the bottom with Snell's Window at the top and Snell's Circle in between. The orange and yellow layers are the most obvious but the other parts of the spectrum are shown in the small insert. The ill-defined blue/grey areas at both upper corners are trees some distance away

wings to the body. As the wings pass through Snell's Circle they may well be tinged with the yellow and orange bands and show what has sometimes been described as 'wing flash'. This would probably not occur with mayflies with dark wings, such as the Iron Blue, Blue-winged Olive, Claret Dun, Olive Upright and March Brown. It is also unlikely to occur with many sedges as their wings are light to dark brown and sometimes mottled as well as being close to the insect's body and so are not as obvious coming into Snell's Circle as are the wings of mayflies.

CHAPTER FOUR

Flat or Curved?

As has been hinted at in previous chapters, one of the most important questions about trout vision is whether its picture plane is flat or curved. Is there any evidence to resolve this question?

To my knowledge the earliest attempt at this task was by Francis Ward in his book *Animal Life Under Water*. His first plate is a drawing of a highland loch. In the upper painting the front of the loch has been cut away to reveal a section through the interior. The picture shows the surrounding hills, a boat, a flying and a floating gull, a fisherman on the bank with a large rock behind him and some underwater rocks. The lines from A and B come to a point close to the substratum and I presume illustrate the inverted visual cone of 97°.

The second plate is an attempt to give the fish's view. The window is the pale central circle surrounded by the mirror. The flying gull appears more of less true to size in the centre of the window. Around the window are a number of indistinct images. On the east side is the upper part of the fisherman on the bank with the rock behind which is more or less in the SE segment of the window. On the S side is a vague indication of the top of the hill in the distance and the very top of the sail of the boat in front of it. On the area of mirror on the right hand are reflections of the bank and underwater rocks while on the left is the dark form of the swimming gull marked X – the gull's head appears at the edge of the window, separated from its body by the mirror. It is not clear what the grey arc at the N side of the window is.

The lower illustration shows an under-water view of the scene in the top picture as it appears from the point C. From Animal Life Under Water *by Francis Ward, 1919*

These two plates are accurate illustrations of our current knowledge of fish vision and are very revealing of the accuracy of Ward's scientific work.

Furthermore Ward has a number very interesting drawings and photographs taken underwater using a viewing tank sunk into the bank of a pond.The first drawing of interest shows the appearance from underwater when the subject is partially above and partially below the surface. The fisherman is wading and the lower of the two drawings shows what the fish would see. The top of the fisherman would appear in the window and two pairs of legs joined at the water surface (W). Note the reflection of the legs is top-to-bottom inverted; this fact will be explained later in this chapter.

Ward's drawn illustration is amply supported by his photograph of a heron's legs as seen from under-water. The arrow indicated the

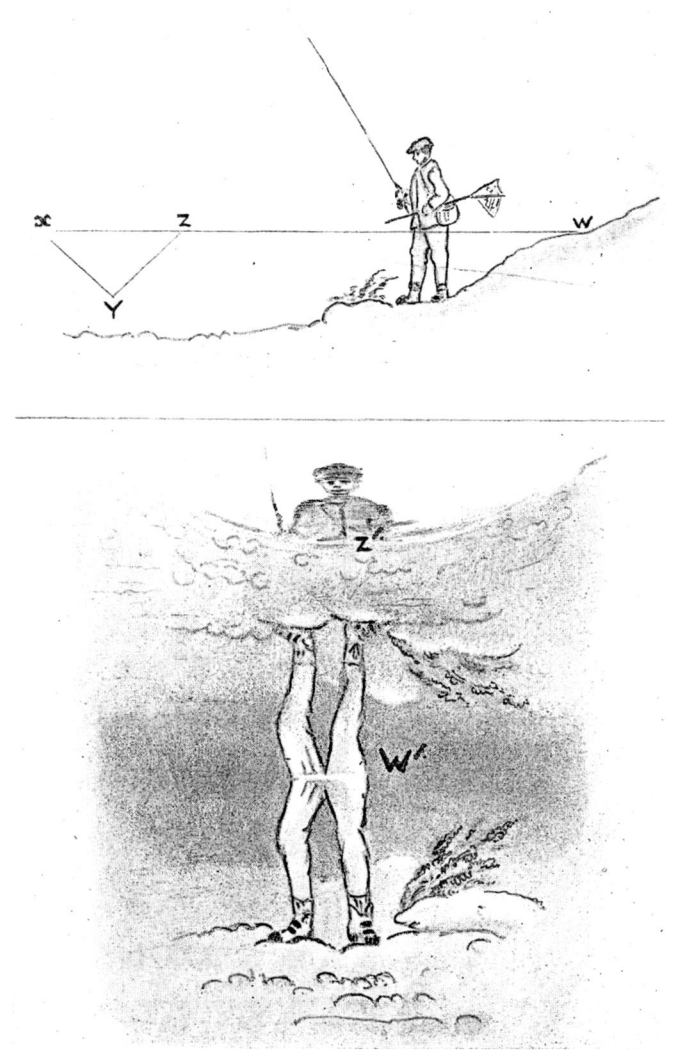

Appearance from under the water, when the subject is partially above and partially below the surface. From Animal Life Under Water *by Francis Ward, 1919*

water surface. The real legs point downwards to the substratum on which the foot rests. The image of the legs reflected in the mirror is top-bottom inverted with the foot at the top of the photo.

Scientifically sound as Ward's observations are, he missed two important points about the mirror and the significance of the

Heron fishing. From Animal Life Under Water *by Francis Ward, 1919*

inverted reflection. Ward does not make reference to the special relationship between mirror and fish, nor the orientation between them. Does the fish see the mirror as a vertical surface or is it angled toward or away from the fish? Ward also misses the significance of the inverted top-bottom reflected image, as have many authors who followed him in writing about fish vision. The significance of the image will be considered later in this chapter.

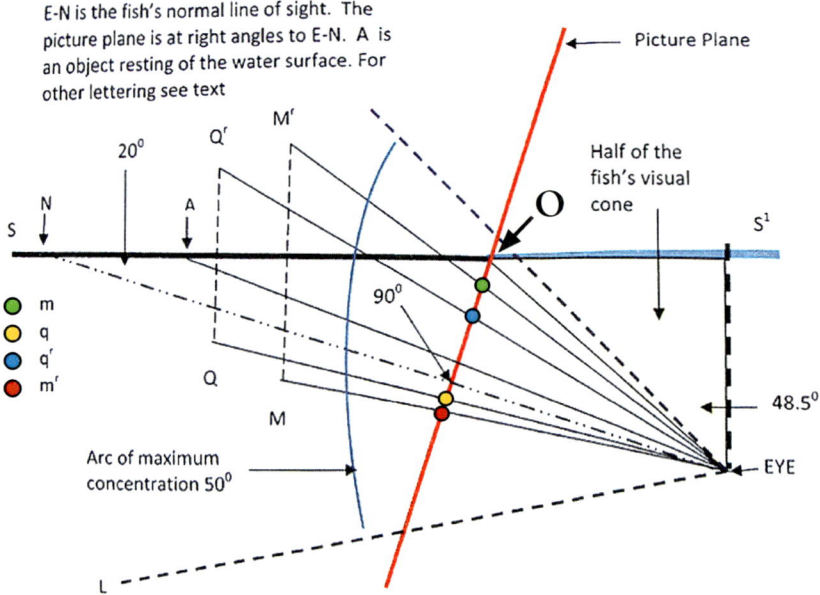

Fig.23 *Re-drawn copy of Harding's illustration (Fig.6) with added colour*

Another book of interest regarding vision in trout is *The Flyfisher and the Trout's Point of View* by Col. E W Harding. This text considers in detail the geometry of the fish's sight and of the rise; the latter, though interesting, is not relevant here. What is relevant is Fig.6, entitled *The Trout's Picture Plane,* which is a two dimensional drawing of various geometrical aspects of trout vision. However some aspects of the diagram are difficult to understand and so I have redrawn the diagram and added colour in the hope of making it more easily understood by the reader

Unfortunately some of the lettering on the diagram is unexplained, either on the drawing itself or in the text. Harding writes 'Points A and objects Q, etc *on the surface of the water* can all be referred to their apparent positions a, q, etc on the picture plane.' However Q is not on the surface of the water but below it. Furthermore Harding nowhere explains why points Q and M lying below the water surface are projected above the water as Q^r and M^r. The only explanation I can see is that Q and M are real objects suspended in the water column which are reflected in the horizontally flat surface mirror; these reflections would appear to be as far above the water as the objects are beneath it.

Looking at oneself in a plane mirror, one's image appears to be as far from the mirror as you are. Lines from, Q/Q^r and M/M^r are projected onto the picture plane as q and m and q^r and m^r. All this is puzzling because all the objects shown as capital letters (Q, M, Q^r and M^r) must surely be invisible to the trout because they are beyond the picture plane, i.e., over the horizon in our terms. Only A is understandable because it *is on the water surface* (S/O/S^1).

Putting aside these minor problems of lettering, Harding's contribution to fish vision was his introduction of the concept of a picture plane in the landscape of the fish. This idea is useful because it relates to human vision. As Harding states 'ordinarily a man looks more or less in a horizontal direction, and quite unconsciously, we refer the positions to all objects on to an imaginary vertical plane between ourselves and them.' When we look in another direction the picture plane moves with us and remains vertical.

However there is another problem with Harding's Fig.6. The picture plane (red in my diagram) is projected into the sky. Can this be the case? When the trout looks skyward is there any need for a picture plane. Figs 13 and 14 in Chapter 3 indicate that the mirror ends at the periphery of the window and the 160° of vision above the water is funnelled down to an inverted cone of 97.5° at the fish's eye. Consequently it would be reasonable to conclude the mirror would end at the point O in Harding's Fig.6 and would not need to be carried on into the air above the window.

If the above comments on certain aspects of Harding's Fig. 6 are correct, then a three dimensional diagram would approximate to Fig.24. The illustration is labelled but reveals some interesting points. A fly floating with the current from A to B to C would not appear to be moving from left to right from the trout's point of view. Rather they would appear to be moving from below *upwards* towards the window. When the fly arrives at D it would have gone through Snell's Circle, perhaps reflecting some of the colours in the ring, and appear

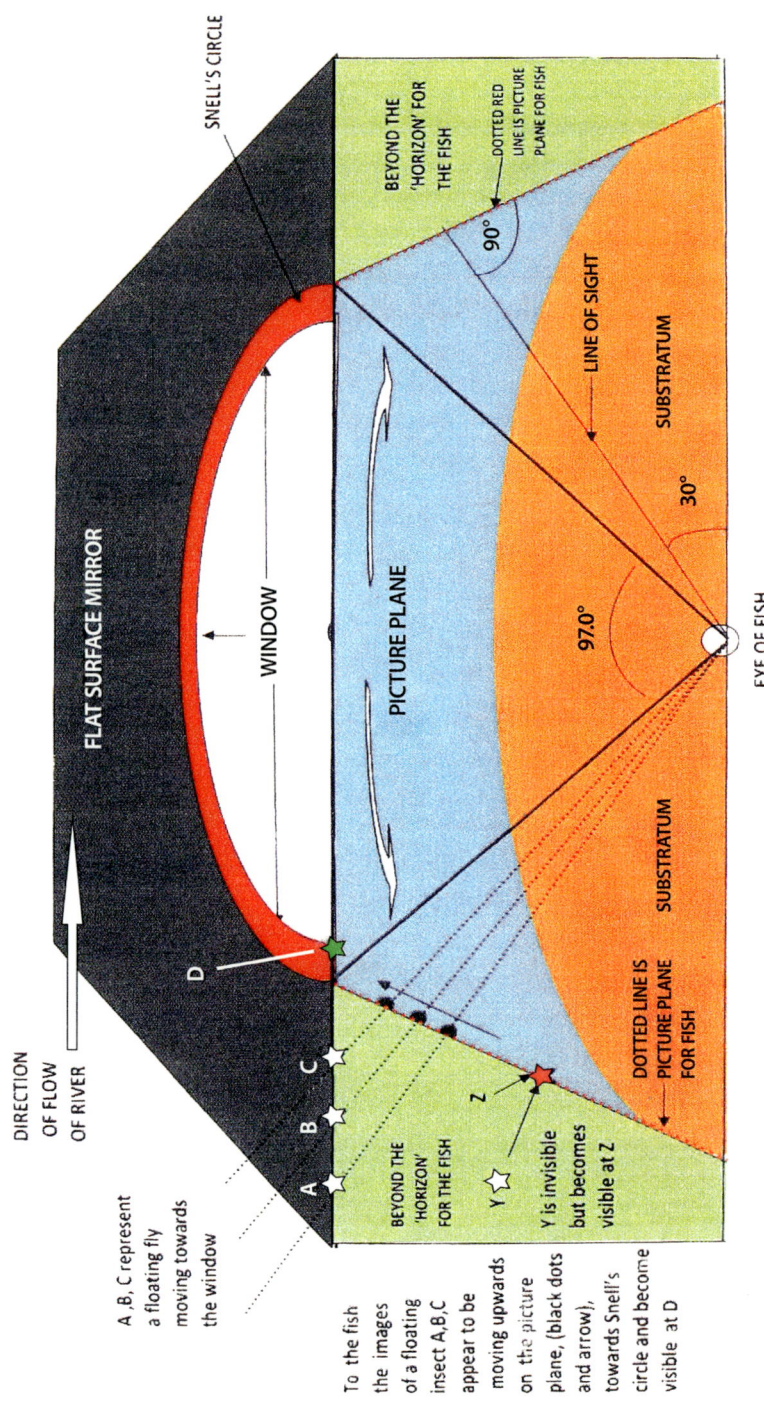

DIRECTION
OF FLOW
OF RIVER

A ,B, C represent
a floating fly
moving towards
the window

FLAT SURFACE MIRROR

SNELL'S CIRCLE

WINDOW

BEYOND THE
'HORIZON' FOR
THE FISH

DOTTED RED
LINE IS PICTURE PLANE FOR FISH

90°

LINE OF SIGHT

SUBSTRATUM

30°

97.0°

PICTURE PLANE

EYE OF FISH

SUBSTRATUM

DOTTED LINE IS
PICTURE PLANE
FOR FISH

Z

Y

Y is invisible
but becomes
visible at Z

BEYOND THE
'HORIZON'
FOR THE FISH

A B C

D

To the fish
the images
of a floating
insect A,B,C
appear to be
moving upwards
on the picture
plane, (black dots
and arrow),
towards Snell's
circle and become
visible at D

46

Fig.24 3D construction of trout's view of its environment above and below the water based on Harding's Fig. 6. This diagram applies to only ONE eye

as a fully recognisable food item. A would show sparkles of light from the insects feet; B, wing flare; and C, fusion of body and wings.

The mirror would be in the form of a flat plane curved around the fish, starting at the rim of the window and extending down to the substratum. Any object beyond the mirror would not be visible to the fish as it would be over its 'horizon.' However a point must be made here and has been mentioned before, namely that the mirror may not be 'silvered.' In all his coloured illustrations Harding shows the mirror in various shades of green; it may possibly be in shades of brown or an admixture of brown and green as well as other colours reflected from the substratum. Consequently the fish may be able to see beyond the mirror but objects would appear indistinct and rather formless.

Fig.24 appears to be a reasonable representation of the fish's view of its environment and knits together our present knowledge of the various aspects of the fish vision into a coherent picture. However there is one situation with which the trout will have to deal which cannot be derived from Harding's Fig.6. How does a fish see an object such as a nymph which is underwater somewhere in the area between the fish and the picture plane? Does the fish see a reflected image of the nymph which is left-right reversed as we do when looking at ourselves in a plane mirror? This reversal is also the reason why ambulances have this word reversed on their front so that when looking in our car mirror we can read the word AMBULANCE. Furthermore does the picture plane have sufficient 'reflectivity' to make a nymph image visible to the fish with any degree of clarity?

Harding in his book has a Plate 1, a sort of frontispiece. In Harding's explanation of this painting he states it is of a view seen by a fish 'some six and a half inches from the centre' (of the picture) and the fish is about 'about four and a half inches below the surface and is looking *through* the water.' Harding continues 'Just below the edge of the window in the centre of the picture is a foreshortened nymph. This is the reflection of the nymph seen at the bottom of the picture and this nymph is a little over ten inches from the fish.' Harding goes on to explain other aspects of his drawing, all of which are understandable but are not relevant here.

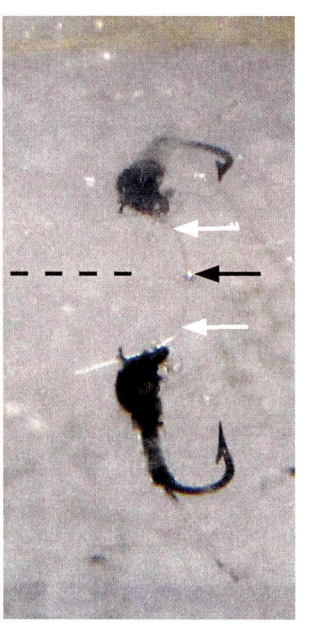

*Fig.25 Artificial nymph as seen in a viewing tank.
The lower image is the object, that is the nymph and its hook, and the upper image is its reflection. The upper image is clearly top-bottom reversed. The dotted black line is the water surface, the black arrow points to where the leader enters the water (small white dot) and the white arrows point to the leader itself and its reflection. The image is slightly fore-shortened as the object is somewhere beyond C (see Fig.27). If the object had been at C the image would have been the same size but if the object were between C & F the image would be larger*

However when mentioning the nymph and its mirror image Harding completely misses a very important point which is that the upper image is inverted (Fig.25). Compare this image with Fig.26 where the image has the same orientation as the gold-headed nymph itself. Using a tank, (as did Harding), I have over the years taken many photographs of artificial flies floating on the water surface, and of hatching nymphs (what I call *interface* flies as they are half above and half below the water line – see: LT Threadgold *Dry Flies:An Improved Tying Method*).

Only relatively recently did I decide to take photographs of nymphs below the surface (Fig.25) and I was in for a huge surprise! This is not the image one would have

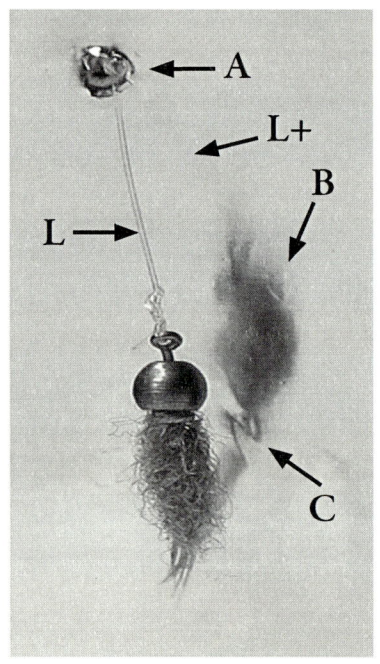

Fig.26 This photograph is of a gold-headed nymph pattern and its reflection. The nymph is suspended by passing the leader L through the hole at A. The mirror is of aluminium foil and angled at about 30° from the vertical. The reflection is at B, and the reflected image of the hook bend at C. The reflection of the leader is vaguely seen at L+. This reflected image is quite different from the reflected image in Fig.25

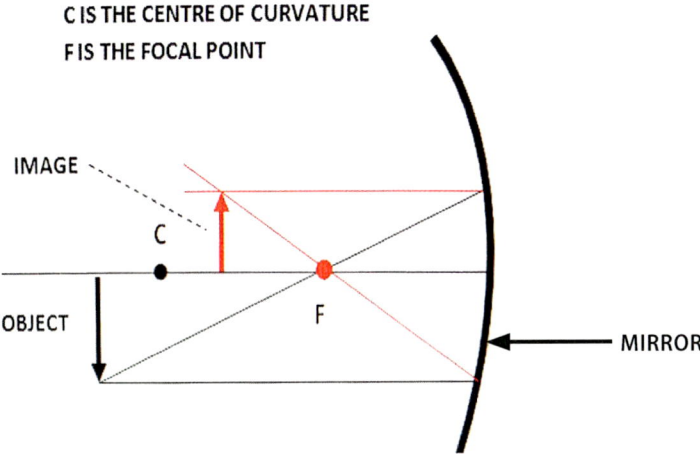

CIS THE CENTRE OF CURVATURE
FIS THE FOCAL POINT

IMAGE

C

OBJECT

F

MIRROR

Fig.27 Image formation of an object using a concave mirror. To make it easier to appreciate Fig.25 the object (artificial nymph) has been placed below the line on which C and F are located and so the image appears above that line (red arrow). Usually in such diagrams the object is above the line

expected to see if the mirror was flat. Instead it should appear as shown in Fig.26.

How is the reversed top-bottom (upside-down) image in Fig.25 produced? There is only one answer – the reflection is produced by a concave mirror as in Fig.27.

I have found a number of authors including Col. E W Harding (*The Flyfisher and the Trout's Point of View*), Francis Ward (*Animal Life Under Water*), Vincent Marinaro (*In the Ring of the Rise*), and Clarke and Goddard (*The Trout and the Fly*) who have in their texts photographs or drawings illustrating upside-down image reflections, and doubtless there are other books showing this type of image. Harding's Plate 1 shows a nymph head-up at the bottom of the plate and its reflection head-down and foreshortened, as in Fig.25.

Fig.28 (overleaf) illustrates that a fly pattern which is an 'interface type', i.e., partly out of and partly in the water, would also show a reversed reflected image.

All these books assume the mirror is a flat plane. Clarke and Goddard call the trout's surroundings a 'bell tent' which could have curved sides but state in their next sentence it is 'very like a

Fig.28 Artificial fly pattern of a still–born sedge with shuck still attached. The upper photograph is the fly on the bench, the middle one the fly resting on the water surface, and the lower one as the fish would see it in the mirror. The reversed image of hook and shuck are clearly evident

cinema screen sloping down in the near middle distance.' Cinema screens are flat, or if panoramic only curved in a single plane. In view of the factors outlined above this idea must be mistaken. The mirror is a curved arc between water surface and substratum though it is not clear the extent of the curvature. A reasonable assumption would be that the centre of the arc is the fish's eye and its view would be similar to that shown in Fig.29. The advantage of this for the trout is that whenever it looked at different parts of the mirror, it would not have to refocus. The whole of the mirror would be in focus all the time, a great advantage. What is unknown is what changes might occur to the mirror's curvature with changes in the depth at which the trout was lying and what differences this makes to the fish's underwater vision.

Fig.29 would make the fish's view of its world similar to our own, i.e., as though it were in an inverted bowl but with mirror like walls, an horizon beyond which it cannot see and with only a limited clear circular area at the top of the bowl. However it should be emphasised that Fig.29 shows only half of the fish's visual field. There is another identical bowl for the other eye and these two bowls overlap (see Figs 10 and 11). Nevertheless this model would fit all the aspects of fish vision from anatomy, histology, view of the above and below-water world in which the trout lives and has its being.

How does the trout see an approaching floating insect? It sees it not on the surface but on its curved picture plane though still in the well known sequence of light spots due to the depressing of the

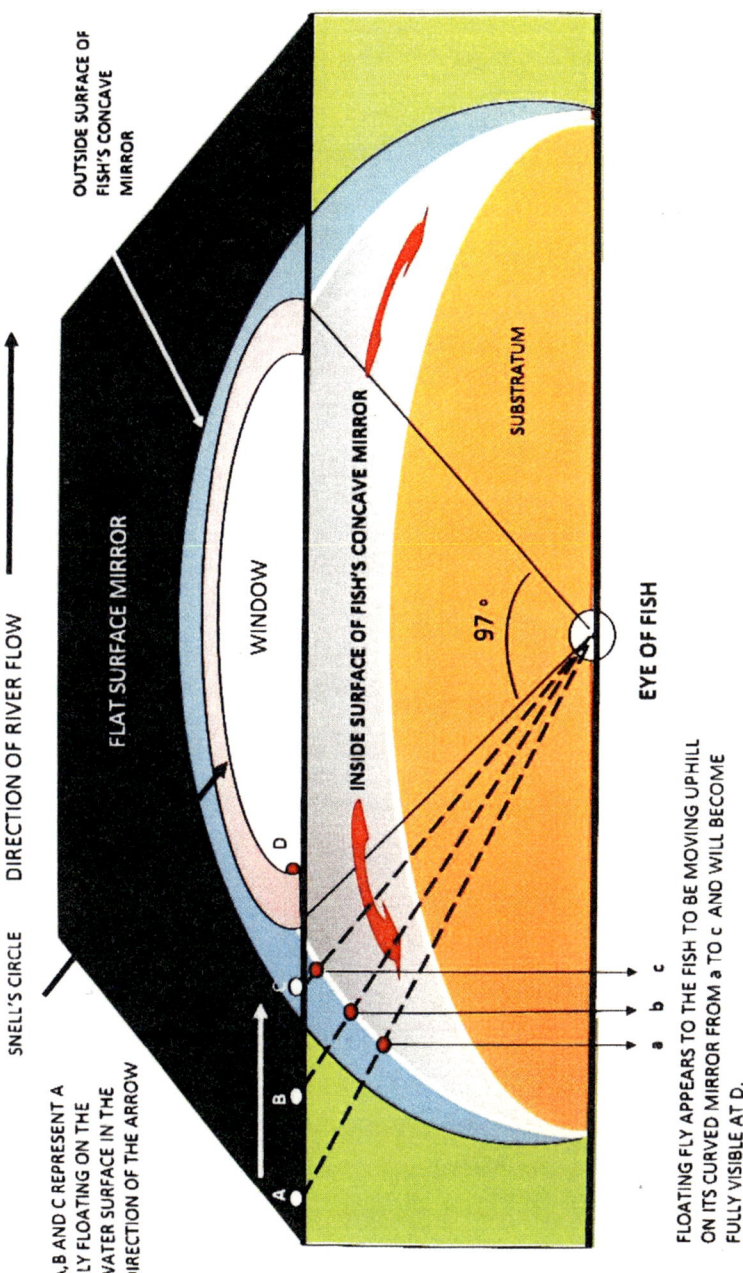

SNELL'S CIRCLE   DIRECTION OF RIVER FLOW

OUTSIDE SURFACE OF FISH'S CONCAVE MIRROR

A,B AND C REPRESENT A FLY FLOATING ON THE WATER SURFACE IN THE DIRECTION OF THE ARROW

FLAT SURFACE MIRROR

WINDOW

INSIDE SURFACE OF FISH'S CONCAVE MIRROR

97°

SUBSTRATUM

EYE OF FISH

FLOATING FLY APPEARS TO THE FISH TO BE MOVING UPHILL ON ITS CURVED MIRROR FROM a TO c AND WILL BECOME FULLY VISIBLE AT D.

Fig.29 Trout's view by ONE eye of its environment if the mirror was a concave one but in other aspects its view would be similar to Fig.19

51

surface film by the insect's feet, followed by the appearance of wings and then, as the insect floats close to Snell's Circle, the body wings and feet unite and the whole insect is seen (D in Fig.29). However though in Fig.29 the insect on the water surface would appear to be going from left to right, (A>B>C) this is not how the trout sees it. To the trout the successive stages of an insect floating towards the window are seen first towards the bottom of the picture plane and then progressively upwards towards the margin of the window (a>b>c in Fig.29). This may appear strange but is inevitable if the mirror surrounds the trout like an upturned bowl with silvered sides and open top, the window.

How is a fully submerged insect, for example a nymph, larva or shrimp, seen by the trout? Since the trout has an horizon (the green areas in Figs 24 and 29), anything in this area cannot be seen by the trout. Only if the object touches the far side of the curved mirror, so causing a distortion of the surface, will the trout be aware of it. However once the object is within the bowl it will be very visible provided the water is clear and will have its reflection in the mirror, that is the trout will see two identical objects, one the actual object and the other its reflection.

Fig.30

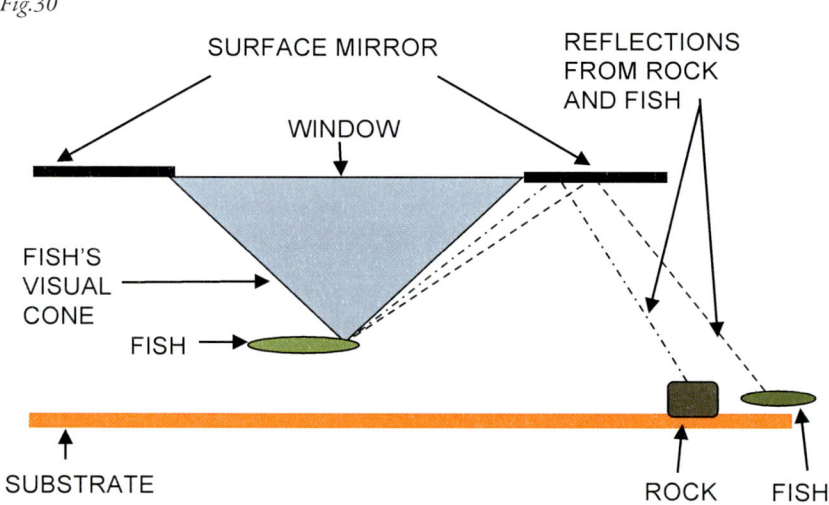

SURFACE MIRROR

REFLECTIONS FROM ROCK AND FISH

WINDOW

FISH'S VISUAL CONE

FISH

SUBSTRATE

ROCK   FISH

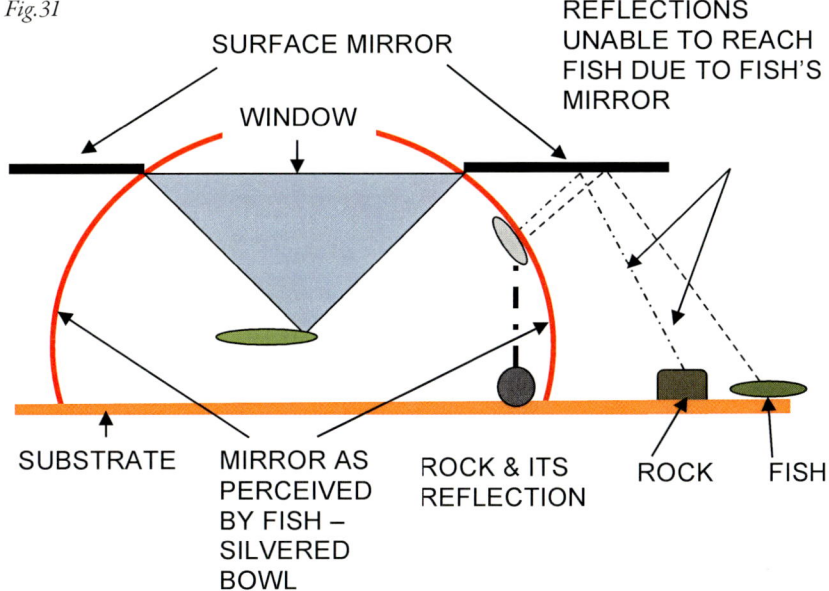

Fig.31

SURFACE MIRROR

WINDOW

REFLECTIONS UNABLE TO REACH FISH DUE TO FISH'S MIRROR

SUBSTRATE   MIRROR AS PERCEIVED BY FISH – SILVERED BOWL   ROCK & ITS REFLECTION   ROCK   FISH

It is common to read in books on fish vision that a trout can see objects outside its visual cone, such as a rock or another fish, due to the light from that object bouncing off the underside of the flat surface mirror into the trout's eyes (Fig.30). If Col. Harding's theory of a picture plane, whether flat or curved, is correct, then this cannot be the case. For the trout the flat surface mirror has transmuted into the picture plane, i.e., the curved silver side of the bowl which has an horizon. This silvered bowl acts as a barrier to any light reflected from the flat surface mirror reaching the fish (Fig.22). Consequently there is no flat surface mirror as far as the trout is concerned. The trout cannot see round corners, as it were. If the object is outside the bowl it does not exist! It is true that any object, such as a rock or another fish, which is within the bowl will be reflected on the picture plane and the trout will see 'two images' as already mentioned (Fig.31).

CHAPTER FIVE

Epilogue

The object of writing this book was so that fly fishermen could look at the world of the trout through its eyes and realise the limitations and specialisations that those eyes possess. Though sight is thought to be the major sense which trout use to hunt their prey, it must not be forgotten that smell, hearing, and taste also play a part, though it is not clear the relative importance of these senses. It should not be forgotten that sight is also important so that trout can avoid and escape their natural enemies such as herons, pike or otters to name but three.

However, with the knowledge gained from this text, what would we see if we were a trout? Our visual world would be a double inverted bowl with 'silvered' sides, (I have used 'silvered' in quotes because the surface will probably be some shades of green or brown). The bowls will overlap to an extent determined by how close we are to the surface. We will have a figure-of-eight, un-silvered 'hole' at the top, the windows (though we have two windows as it were, this configuration will be called 'the window'). Through this window we can see the environment above-the-water to a limited extent. Objects in that above-water world would be distorted at the edge of the window, get progressively more defined and true to size, shape and colour as they approached the centre of the window, but would appear to be projected into the air for a distance determined by the closeness of the above-water object.

In strong light anything coming into our window will appear black or so dark that the colour of the object may not be evident or strongly expressed. In dimmer light colours will be more evident. This may be one of the reasons why we feed more actively late in the day, the well-known evening rise. An additional factor would be the change-over of our eyes from day to night vision due to the migration of the rods and cones. The addition of colour to the details of the outline of the food material may induce us to rise and take which we might not do to an outline alone.

Our surrounding bowls, being centred on us, move when we move. Consequently objects in the water which, when we are in one position are on the far side of the mirror, that is beyond the 'horizon,' suddenly come into view as we and the bowls move. These immersed objects would suddenly break through the mirror and become visible and while they are close to the curved mirror they would be reflected as images which are inverted, i.e., we would see two nymphs, one upside-down. The fracturing of the mirror in these localised areas as objects such as nymphs or larvae, a piece of flotsam, a clump of weed or a rock on the substratum passes from outside the bowls to inside would be very obvious and attract our attention. The sudden presence of a nymph or larva entering our bowls would be of special interest and probably stimulate our hunting instinct. In some way our visual system would deal with the double image in the mirror and so allow us to judge which is the edible object and which its mirror image, or that both objects are inedible and so let them pass by.

So, though in one area of our mirror objects would appear quite suddenly, others on the opposite side would break through the mirror and disappear. The mirror could quite possibly be frequently disrupted and fractured by objects large and small breaking into and then out of our area of view because they floated on or were immersed in the water current of a river; in a lake the interruptions might be less frequent.

Another phenomenon we would notice if we were a trout is that our bowls would not stay the same size. Depending on the depth of water in which we were swimming the bowl would become larger as we went deeper and the window would have a larger diameter. As we rose towards the surface the bowl would narrow and the window shrink in size though the bowls would still contact the substratum. Of course we would not be aware of this!

Furthermore we would not be able to see the full internal volume of the bowl because of the blind spots which would lie close to us like a cloak. We would not be aware of our dorsal surface, dorsal fin, our face, most of our ventral surface and most of our tail, though we might catch a brief glance of our tail as we waved it to swim and might also be aware of our lateral fins. Whether or not the cloak would contact the substratum at all depths we might be swimming at is not clear. For us humans our cloak seems to have no boundary, but then we do not have eyes with 180° arc of monocular vision for each eye.

Finally how would we see our prey? If the nymph, larva, shrimp or small fish were within the area of water encompassed by our upturned bowls then we would see such prey in either of the two monocular zones of vision or if more or less straight ahead of us we would see it with our binocular vision. With our monocular zone of vision we might not be able to judge accurately the distance to the prey item, or the speed it was moving, and the object might be a somewhat vague image at the extreme edges of this monocular zone. However we could easily correct this circumstance by turning in the water and bringing the object into the binocular zone where we could better judge distance and speed of movement. Clearly our monocular and binocular vision would give us an excellent all-round view of our underwater world within the bowls.

What about prey items in the air or floating on the water system? If an aerial object came within the radius of the window we could see it, and if we turned to use our zone of binocular vision we should be able to judge its height above the water surface, and its speed and direction. If we judged the aerial prey item was within our 'jumping distance' we might have a go at capturing it in mid-air. Certainly a trout which launches itself into the air to take a prey is one of the more spectacular actions of trout which regularly excites the flyfisher's attention; it is a happening which tends to stick in the memory!

What about the prey object floating towards us on the surface film? The first sign of a prey item we would notice would be a set of sparkling dots in our mirror due to the feet of the insect indenting the surface film; the insect's footprint as it were. This first image would continue to float towards us until the tips of the wings projected into the window, i.e., were more that 10° from the horizontal. The wings would be visible before the body because the latter would still be below or close to the 10° from the horizontal. The wings would get progressively larger and we would see the footprint and wings at the same time. Finally as the insect reached Snell's Circle and moved into the edge of the window, we would then see the body had joined the wings and footprint to give a vision of the entire insect. If the wings were nearly translucent or pale in colour, there might be some colouring of the wings as they passed through Snell's Circle – so-called wing flash.

Though this sequence of events is well known it is not how we as a trout would see it. Diagrams often show the floating fly moving from left to right or the reverse in the direction of the window but for us these images would move on our curved mirror from the substratum upwards towards the window (Figs 16 & 20 in Chapter 4). This may seem unexpected to the reader but not to us the trout!

It has been frequently stated that we must have excellent sight to survive in a milieu with such uncertain properties. Would that sight be equal to or exceed digital photograph from a camera with about 12 million pixels? The following four images are just such digital photographs and reveal some surprising features. The photographs are of a footprint-patterned artificial mayfly taken in a viewing tank. The fine line across the top of all photos is a silk thread used to keep the fly still and each photo is progressively nearer our window.

The bracketed zone in each photo is Snell's Circle and shows some yellowish, reddish and blue lines. In the first photo the fly is close to Snell's Circle and the wings are very clear. Below is the attached body (white arrow) and towards the bottom are the sparkles produced by the hackles (thick white arrow). The second photo shows the feet (white arrow) and the wings and body clearly and the black arrow

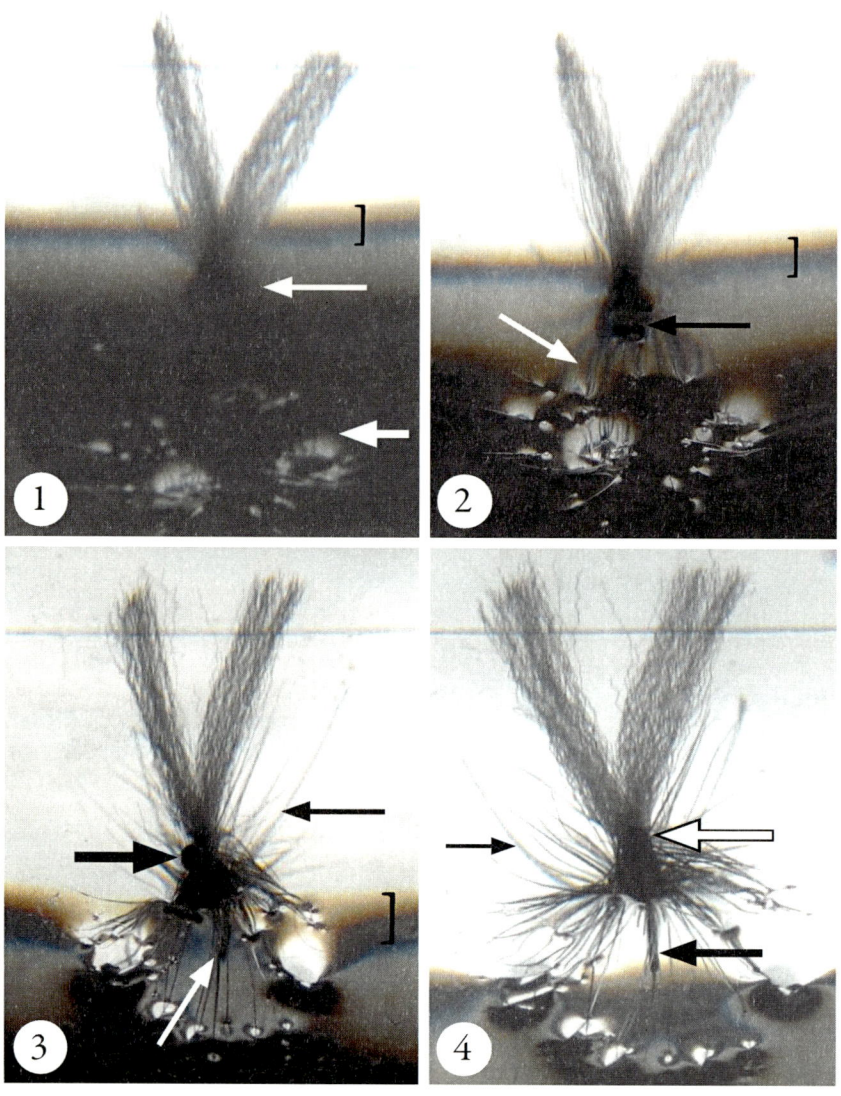

points to the eye of the hook. The hackle 'legs' arise from the base of the body but the foot sparkles are also still evident and detached.

In photograph 3 the hook eye is visible at the thick black arrow, the above the body hackles at the black arrow and the footprints, legs and body are combined. The white arrow points to the hook barb. In photo 4 the fly is just at the border of our window. The small black arrow points to the tail, the heavy black arrow to the hook barb and the hollow arrow to the hook eye. The hackle 'legs' are very clear and too numerous for a real fly as are the above-the-body hackles. However in all these photographs an important element is missing, namely the leader connected to the hook eye, which would appear as a dark line, a very evident feature.

If we as a trout can see details such as those revealed by these photographs, it is surprising that we do not know instinctively that this floating fly is a fake. So why do we take such imitations? It may be that there are sufficient clues in the pattern to stimulate our hunting instinct, though we have no idea how many or which clues these may be. Perhaps we ignore the extraneous features of the artificial because we are concentrating on aspects which interest us most or which 'look right' for the insect being imitated. These photos were of course taken in still water conditions, a situation rarely observed by a trout. There are always features of water, whether in a river or lake, which will disturb or distort the image we see but there may still be some feature to attract, say the wings or the colour. Taking in mind all these conditions it is surprising that the fly fisherman is as successful at capturing us as he is!

References

Goddard, John & Clarke, Brian. *The Trout and the Fly*. Ernest Benn, London, 1980.

Harding, E W. *The Flyfisher and the Trout's Point of View*. Seeley Service, London, 1931.

Marinaro, Vincent C. *In the Ring of the Rise*. Crown Publishers, New York, 1976.

Pumphrey, R J. *Concerning Vision*. (In Ramsey J.A. & Wigglesworth V.B. *The Cell and the Organism*. Cambridge University Press, Cambridge, 1961).

Randall, Jason. *Trout Sense: A Fly Fisher's Guide to What Trout See, Hear and Smell*. Stackpole Books, Mechanicsburg, Pennsylvania, 2014.

Schullery, Paul. *The Rise: Streamside Observations on Trout, Flies, and Fly Fishing*. Stackpole Books, Mechanicsburg, Pennsylvania, 2006.

Sosin, M & Clarke, J. *Through The Fish's Eye: An Angler's Guide to Fish Behaviour*. Andre Deutsch, London, 1976.

Threadgold, Lawrence T. *Dry Flies: An Improved Method of Tying*. Swan Hill Press, Shrewsbury, 1999.

Ward, Francis. *Animal Life Under Water*. Cassell, London, 1919.

Index